35 Pudding Recipes for Home

By: Kelly Johnson

Table of Contents

- Chocolate Pudding
- Vanilla Pudding
- Butterscotch Pudding
- Rice Pudding
- Tapioca Pudding
- Bread Pudding
- Banana Pudding
- Lemon Pudding
- Coconut Pudding
- Pumpkin Pudding
- Caramel Pudding
- Mocha Pudding
- Almond Pudding
- Gingerbread Pudding
- Strawberry Pudding
- Spiced Pudding
- Eggnog Pudding
- Maple Pudding
- Chia Seed Pudding
- Peanut Butter Pudding
- Raspberry Pudding
- Mint Chocolate Pudding
- Coffee Pudding
- White Chocolate Pudding
- Pistachio Pudding
- Malted Milk Pudding
- Matcha Pudding
- Apple Pudding
- Cheesecake Pudding
- Chocolate Mint Pudding
- Carrot Pudding
- Fig Pudding

- Cherry Pudding
- Date Pudding
- Nutella Pudding

Chocolate Pudding

- 2 cups whole milk
- 1/2 cup granulated sugar
- 1/4 cup unsweetened cocoa powder
- 1/4 cup cornstarch
- 1/4 tsp salt
- 1/4 cup water
- 1 tsp vanilla extract

Instructions:

1. **Mix Dry Ingredients:** In a medium saucepan, whisk together sugar, cocoa powder, cornstarch, and salt.
2. **Combine Liquids:** Gradually whisk in milk and water until smooth.
3. **Cook Pudding:** Cook over medium heat, whisking constantly until the mixture thickens and starts to bubble (about 5-7 minutes).
4. **Add Vanilla:** Remove from heat and stir in vanilla extract.
5. **Chill:** Pour into serving dishes and chill in the refrigerator for at least 2 hours before serving.

Vanilla Pudding

- 2 cups whole milk
- 1/2 cup granulated sugar
- 1/4 cup cornstarch
- 1/4 tsp salt
- 1 tsp vanilla extract

Instructions:

1. **Mix Dry Ingredients:** In a medium saucepan, whisk together sugar, cornstarch, and salt.
2. **Combine Liquids:** Gradually whisk in milk until smooth.
3. **Cook Pudding:** Cook over medium heat, whisking constantly until the mixture thickens and starts to bubble (about 5-7 minutes).
4. **Add Vanilla:** Remove from heat and stir in vanilla extract.
5. **Chill:** Pour into serving dishes and refrigerate for at least 2 hours before serving.

Butterscotch Pudding

- 2 cups whole milk
- 1/2 cup packed brown sugar
- 1/4 cup cornstarch
- 1/4 tsp salt
- 1/4 cup unsalted butter
- 1 tsp vanilla extract

Instructions:

1. **Mix Dry Ingredients:** In a medium saucepan, whisk together brown sugar, cornstarch, and salt.
2. **Combine Liquids:** Gradually whisk in milk until smooth.
3. **Cook Pudding:** Cook over medium heat, whisking constantly until the mixture thickens and starts to bubble (about 5-7 minutes).
4. **Add Butter and Vanilla:** Remove from heat and stir in butter and vanilla extract.
5. **Chill:** Pour into serving dishes and chill in the refrigerator for at least 2 hours before serving.

Rice Pudding

- 1/2 cup uncooked short-grain rice
- 2 cups whole milk
- 1/2 cup granulated sugar
- 1/4 cup heavy cream
- 1/2 tsp vanilla extract
- 1/4 tsp ground cinnamon (optional)
- 1/4 tsp salt

Instructions:

1. **Cook Rice:** In a medium saucepan, combine rice and milk. Cook over medium heat until the rice is tender and the mixture has thickened, about 20-25 minutes. Stir frequently.
2. **Add Sugar and Cream:** Stir in sugar, heavy cream, and salt. Continue cooking for 5-10 minutes until the mixture is creamy.
3. **Add Vanilla:** Remove from heat and stir in vanilla extract.
4. **Chill:** Pour into serving dishes and let cool before refrigerating. Chill for at least 2 hours before serving.

Tapioca Pudding

- 1/2 cup small pearl tapioca
- 2 3/4 cups whole milk
- 1/2 cup granulated sugar
- 1/4 tsp salt
- 1 tsp vanilla extract

Instructions:

1. **Soak Tapioca:** Soak tapioca in 1 cup of milk for at least 30 minutes.
2. **Cook Tapioca:** In a medium saucepan, combine soaked tapioca, remaining milk, sugar, and salt. Cook over medium heat, stirring constantly until the mixture thickens and tapioca becomes translucent (about 15-20 minutes).
3. **Add Vanilla:** Remove from heat and stir in vanilla extract.
4. **Chill:** Pour into serving dishes and let cool. Chill in the refrigerator for at least 2 hours before serving.

Bread Pudding

- 4 cups cubed day-old bread
- 2 cups whole milk
- 1/2 cup granulated sugar
- 2 large eggs
- 1/4 cup unsalted butter, melted
- 1 tsp vanilla extract
- 1/2 tsp ground cinnamon
- 1/4 tsp ground nutmeg

Instructions:

1. **Preheat Oven:** Preheat your oven to 350°F (175°C).
2. **Prepare Bread:** Place cubed bread in a large bowl.
3. **Mix Wet Ingredients:** In another bowl, whisk together milk, sugar, eggs, melted butter, vanilla extract, cinnamon, and nutmeg.
4. **Combine and Bake:** Pour the mixture over the bread cubes, stirring to combine. Let sit for 10 minutes. Pour into a greased baking dish and bake for 45-50 minutes, or until set and golden brown.
5. **Cool and Serve:** Let cool slightly before serving.

Banana Pudding

- 3 cups whole milk
- 1/2 cup granulated sugar
- 1/4 cup cornstarch
- 1/4 tsp salt
- 1 tsp vanilla extract
- 3 ripe bananas, sliced
- 1 cup vanilla wafers

Instructions:

1. **Mix Dry Ingredients:** In a medium saucepan, whisk together sugar, cornstarch, and salt.
2. **Combine Liquids:** Gradually whisk in milk until smooth.
3. **Cook Pudding:** Cook over medium heat, whisking constantly until the mixture thickens and starts to bubble (about 5-7 minutes).
4. **Add Vanilla:** Remove from heat and stir in vanilla extract.
5. **Layer and Chill:** In a serving dish, layer pudding, banana slices, and vanilla wafers. Repeat layers and finish with pudding. Chill in the refrigerator for at least 2 hours before serving.

Lemon Pudding

- 2 cups whole milk
- 1/2 cup granulated sugar
- 1/4 cup cornstarch
- 1/4 tsp salt
- 1/4 cup fresh lemon juice (about 2 lemons)
- 1 tbsp lemon zest

Instructions:

1. **Mix Dry Ingredients:** In a medium saucepan, whisk together sugar, cornstarch, and salt.
2. **Combine Liquids:** Gradually whisk in milk until smooth.
3. **Cook Pudding:** Cook over medium heat, whisking constantly until the mixture thickens and starts to bubble (about 5-7 minutes).
4. **Add Lemon:** Remove from heat and stir in lemon juice and lemon zest.
5. **Chill:** Pour into serving dishes and refrigerate for at least 2 hours before serving.

Coconut Pudding

- 2 cups whole milk
- 1 cup coconut milk
- 1/2 cup granulated sugar
- 1/4 cup cornstarch
- 1/4 tsp salt
- 1/2 cup shredded coconut (sweetened or unsweetened)
- 1 tsp vanilla extract

Instructions:

1. **Mix Dry Ingredients:** In a medium saucepan, whisk together sugar, cornstarch, and salt.
2. **Combine Liquids:** Gradually whisk in whole milk and coconut milk until smooth.
3. **Cook Pudding:** Cook over medium heat, whisking constantly until the mixture thickens and starts to bubble (about 5-7 minutes).
4. **Add Coconut and Vanilla:** Stir in shredded coconut and vanilla extract.
5. **Chill:** Pour into serving dishes and refrigerate for at least 2 hours before serving.

Pumpkin Pudding

- 2 cups whole milk
- 1/2 cup pumpkin puree
- 1/2 cup granulated sugar
- 1/4 cup cornstarch
- 1/4 tsp salt
- 1/2 tsp ground cinnamon
- 1/4 tsp ground nutmeg
- 1/4 tsp ground ginger
- 1/2 tsp vanilla extract

Instructions:

1. **Mix Dry Ingredients:** In a medium saucepan, whisk together sugar, cornstarch, salt, cinnamon, nutmeg, and ginger.
2. **Combine Liquids:** Gradually whisk in milk and pumpkin puree until smooth.
3. **Cook Pudding:** Cook over medium heat, whisking constantly until the mixture thickens and starts to bubble (about 5-7 minutes).
4. **Add Vanilla:** Remove from heat and stir in vanilla extract.
5. **Chill:** Pour into serving dishes and refrigerate for at least 2 hours before serving.

Caramel Pudding

- 2 cups whole milk
- 1/2 cup granulated sugar
- 1/4 cup brown sugar
- 1/4 cup cornstarch
- 1/4 tsp salt
- 1/4 cup water
- 1/4 cup unsalted butter
- 1 tsp vanilla extract

Instructions:

1. **Caramelize Sugar:** In a medium saucepan, heat granulated sugar over medium heat until it melts and turns a deep amber color, swirling the pan occasionally. Remove from heat.
2. **Combine Liquid Ingredients:** In a separate bowl, whisk together brown sugar, cornstarch, and salt. Gradually whisk in milk.
3. **Combine and Cook:** Slowly whisk the milk mixture into the caramelized sugar. Return to heat and cook over medium heat, whisking constantly until thickened (about 5-7 minutes).
4. **Add Butter and Vanilla:** Remove from heat and stir in butter and vanilla extract.
5. **Chill:** Pour into serving dishes and refrigerate for at least 2 hours before serving.

Mocha Pudding

- 2 cups whole milk
- 1/2 cup granulated sugar
- 1/4 cup unsweetened cocoa powder
- 1/4 cup cornstarch
- 1/4 tsp salt
- 2 tbsp brewed coffee (strong)
- 1 tsp vanilla extract

Instructions:

1. **Mix Dry Ingredients:** In a medium saucepan, whisk together sugar, cocoa powder, cornstarch, and salt.
2. **Combine Liquids:** Gradually whisk in milk and brewed coffee until smooth.
3. **Cook Pudding:** Cook over medium heat, whisking constantly until the mixture thickens and starts to bubble (about 5-7 minutes).
4. **Add Vanilla:** Remove from heat and stir in vanilla extract.
5. **Chill:** Pour into serving dishes and refrigerate for at least 2 hours before serving.

Almond Pudding

- 2 cups whole milk
- 1/2 cup granulated sugar
- 1/4 cup cornstarch
- 1/4 tsp salt
- 1/4 cup almond milk
- 1/2 tsp almond extract
- 1/4 cup sliced almonds (toasted, for garnish)

Instructions:

1. **Mix Dry Ingredients:** In a medium saucepan, whisk together sugar, cornstarch, and salt.
2. **Combine Liquids:** Gradually whisk in whole milk and almond milk until smooth.
3. **Cook Pudding:** Cook over medium heat, whisking constantly until the mixture thickens and starts to bubble (about 5-7 minutes).
4. **Add Almond Extract:** Remove from heat and stir in almond extract.
5. **Chill:** Pour into serving dishes and refrigerate for at least 2 hours before serving. Garnish with toasted sliced almonds before serving.

Gingerbread Pudding

- 2 cups whole milk
- 1/2 cup granulated sugar
- 1/4 cup molasses
- 1/4 cup cornstarch
- 1/4 tsp salt
- 1 tsp ground ginger
- 1/2 tsp ground cinnamon
- 1/4 tsp ground cloves
- 1/2 tsp vanilla extract

Instructions:

1. **Mix Dry Ingredients:** In a medium saucepan, whisk together sugar, cornstarch, salt, ginger, cinnamon, and cloves.
2. **Combine Liquids:** Gradually whisk in milk and molasses until smooth.
3. **Cook Pudding:** Cook over medium heat, whisking constantly until the mixture thickens and starts to bubble (about 5-7 minutes).
4. **Add Vanilla:** Remove from heat and stir in vanilla extract.
5. **Chill:** Pour into serving dishes and refrigerate for at least 2 hours before serving.

Strawberry Pudding

- 2 cups whole milk
- 1/2 cup granulated sugar
- 1/4 cup cornstarch
- 1/4 tsp salt
- 1 cup fresh strawberries, pureed
- 1/2 tsp vanilla extract

Instructions:

1. **Mix Dry Ingredients:** In a medium saucepan, whisk together sugar, cornstarch, and salt.
2. **Combine Liquids:** Gradually whisk in milk until smooth.
3. **Cook Pudding:** Cook over medium heat, whisking constantly until the mixture thickens and starts to bubble (about 5-7 minutes).
4. **Add Strawberry Puree and Vanilla:** Remove from heat and stir in strawberry puree and vanilla extract.
5. **Chill:** Pour into serving dishes and refrigerate for at least 2 hours before serving.

Spiced Pudding

- 2 cups whole milk
- 1/2 cup granulated sugar
- 1/4 cup cornstarch
- 1/4 tsp salt
- 1/2 tsp ground cinnamon
- 1/4 tsp ground nutmeg
- 1/4 tsp ground allspice
- 1/2 tsp vanilla extract

Instructions:

1. **Mix Dry Ingredients:** In a medium saucepan, whisk together sugar, cornstarch, salt, cinnamon, nutmeg, and allspice.
2. **Combine Liquids:** Gradually whisk in milk until smooth.
3. **Cook Pudding:** Cook over medium heat, whisking constantly until the mixture thickens and starts to bubble (about 5-7 minutes).
4. **Add Vanilla:** Remove from heat and stir in vanilla extract.
5. **Chill:** Pour into serving dishes and refrigerate for at least 2 hours before serving.

Eggnog Pudding

- 2 cups whole milk
- 1 cup eggnog
- 1/2 cup granulated sugar
- 1/4 cup cornstarch
- 1/4 tsp salt
- 1/2 tsp ground nutmeg
- 1/2 tsp vanilla extract

Instructions:

1. **Mix Dry Ingredients:** In a medium saucepan, whisk together sugar, cornstarch, salt, and nutmeg.
2. **Combine Liquids:** Gradually whisk in milk and eggnog until smooth.
3. **Cook Pudding:** Cook over medium heat, whisking constantly until the mixture thickens and starts to bubble (about 5-7 minutes).
4. **Add Vanilla:** Remove from heat and stir in vanilla extract.
5. **Chill:** Pour into serving dishes and refrigerate for at least 2 hours before serving.

Maple Pudding

- 2 cups whole milk
- 1/2 cup pure maple syrup
- 1/4 cup granulated sugar
- 1/4 cup cornstarch
- 1/4 tsp salt
- 1 tsp vanilla extract

Instructions:

1. **Mix Dry Ingredients:** In a medium saucepan, whisk together sugar, cornstarch, and salt.
2. **Combine Liquids:** Gradually whisk in milk and maple syrup until smooth.
3. **Cook Pudding:** Cook over medium heat, whisking constantly until the mixture thickens and starts to bubble (about 5-7 minutes).
4. **Add Vanilla:** Remove from heat and stir in vanilla extract.
5. **Chill:** Pour into serving dishes and refrigerate for at least 2 hours before serving.

Chia Seed Pudding

- 1/2 cup chia seeds

- 2 cups whole milk (or almond milk)
- 1/4 cup honey or maple syrup
- 1 tsp vanilla extract
- Fresh fruit or nuts for topping (optional)

Instructions:

1. **Combine Ingredients:** In a bowl, whisk together chia seeds, milk, honey, and vanilla extract.
2. **Chill:** Cover and refrigerate for at least 4 hours or overnight, stirring occasionally.
3. **Serve:** Stir well before serving. Top with fresh fruit or nuts if desired.

Peanut Butter Pudding

- 2 cups whole milk

- 1/2 cup creamy peanut butter
- 1/2 cup granulated sugar
- 1/4 cup cornstarch
- 1/4 tsp salt
- 1/2 tsp vanilla extract

Instructions:

1. **Mix Dry Ingredients:** In a medium saucepan, whisk together sugar, cornstarch, and salt.
2. **Combine Liquids:** Gradually whisk in milk until smooth.
3. **Cook Pudding:** Cook over medium heat, whisking constantly until the mixture thickens and starts to bubble (about 5-7 minutes).
4. **Add Peanut Butter and Vanilla:** Remove from heat and stir in peanut butter and vanilla extract until smooth.
5. **Chill:** Pour into serving dishes and refrigerate for at least 2 hours before serving.

Raspberry Pudding

- 2 cups whole milk

- 1/2 cup granulated sugar
- 1/4 cup cornstarch
- 1/4 tsp salt
- 1 cup fresh raspberries or raspberry puree
- 1/2 tsp vanilla extract

Instructions:

1. **Mix Dry Ingredients:** In a medium saucepan, whisk together sugar, cornstarch, and salt.
2. **Combine Liquids:** Gradually whisk in milk until smooth.
3. **Cook Pudding:** Cook over medium heat, whisking constantly until the mixture thickens and starts to bubble (about 5-7 minutes).
4. **Add Raspberry and Vanilla:** Remove from heat and stir in raspberry puree and vanilla extract.
5. **Chill:** Pour into serving dishes and refrigerate for at least 2 hours before serving.

Mint Chocolate Pudding

- 2 cups whole milk

- 1/2 cup granulated sugar
- 1/4 cup unsweetened cocoa powder
- 1/4 cup cornstarch
- 1/4 tsp salt
- 1/2 tsp mint extract
- 1/2 cup chocolate chips (optional)

Instructions:

1. **Mix Dry Ingredients:** In a medium saucepan, whisk together sugar, cocoa powder, cornstarch, and salt.
2. **Combine Liquids:** Gradually whisk in milk until smooth.
3. **Cook Pudding:** Cook over medium heat, whisking constantly until the mixture thickens and starts to bubble (about 5-7 minutes).
4. **Add Mint Extract and Chocolate:** Remove from heat and stir in mint extract and chocolate chips if using until melted and smooth.
5. **Chill:** Pour into serving dishes and refrigerate for at least 2 hours before serving.

Coffee Pudding

- 2 cups whole milk

- 1/2 cup granulated sugar
- 1/4 cup cornstarch
- 1/4 tsp salt
- 1/4 cup strong brewed coffee
- 1 tsp vanilla extract

Instructions:

1. **Mix Dry Ingredients:** In a medium saucepan, whisk together sugar, cornstarch, and salt.
2. **Combine Liquids:** Gradually whisk in milk and brewed coffee until smooth.
3. **Cook Pudding:** Cook over medium heat, whisking constantly until the mixture thickens and starts to bubble (about 5-7 minutes).
4. **Add Vanilla:** Remove from heat and stir in vanilla extract.
5. **Chill:** Pour into serving dishes and refrigerate for at least 2 hours before serving.

White Chocolate Pudding

- 2 cups whole milk
- 1/2 cup white chocolate chips

- 1/4 cup granulated sugar
- 1/4 cup cornstarch
- 1/4 tsp salt
- 1 tsp vanilla extract

Instructions:

1. **Mix Dry Ingredients:** In a medium saucepan, whisk together sugar, cornstarch, and salt.
2. **Combine Liquids:** Gradually whisk in milk until smooth.
3. **Cook Pudding:** Cook over medium heat, whisking constantly until the mixture thickens and starts to bubble (about 5-7 minutes).
4. **Add White Chocolate and Vanilla:** Remove from heat and stir in white chocolate chips and vanilla extract until smooth.
5. **Chill:** Pour into serving dishes and refrigerate for at least 2 hours before serving.

Pistachio Pudding

- 2 cups whole milk
- 1/2 cup granulated sugar

- 1/4 cup cornstarch
- 1/4 tsp salt
- 1/2 cup pistachio nuts, finely chopped
- 1/2 tsp vanilla extract

Instructions:

1. **Mix Dry Ingredients:** In a medium saucepan, whisk together sugar, cornstarch, and salt.
2. **Combine Liquids:** Gradually whisk in milk until smooth.
3. **Cook Pudding:** Cook over medium heat, whisking constantly until the mixture thickens and starts to bubble (about 5-7 minutes).
4. **Add Pistachios and Vanilla:** Remove from heat and stir in chopped pistachios and vanilla extract.
5. **Chill:** Pour into serving dishes and refrigerate for at least 2 hours before serving.

Malted Milk Pudding

- 2 cups whole milk
- 1/2 cup malted milk powder

- 1/2 cup granulated sugar
- 1/4 cup cornstarch
- 1/4 tsp salt
- 1 tsp vanilla extract

Instructions:

1. **Mix Dry Ingredients:** In a medium saucepan, whisk together sugar, cornstarch, salt, and malted milk powder.
2. **Combine Liquids:** Gradually whisk in milk until smooth.
3. **Cook Pudding:** Cook over medium heat, whisking constantly until the mixture thickens and starts to bubble (about 5-7 minutes).
4. **Add Vanilla:** Remove from heat and stir in vanilla extract.
5. **Chill:** Pour into serving dishes and refrigerate for at least 2 hours before serving.

Matcha Pudding

- 2 cups whole milk
- 1/2 cup granulated sugar

- 1/4 cup cornstarch
- 1/4 tsp salt
- 2 tbsp matcha powder
- 1/2 tsp vanilla extract

Instructions:

1. **Mix Dry Ingredients:** In a medium saucepan, whisk together sugar, cornstarch, salt, and matcha powder.
2. **Combine Liquids:** Gradually whisk in milk until smooth.
3. **Cook Pudding:** Cook over medium heat, whisking constantly until the mixture thickens and starts to bubble (about 5-7 minutes).
4. **Add Vanilla:** Remove from heat and stir in vanilla extract.
5. **Chill:** Pour into serving dishes and refrigerate for at least 2 hours before serving.

Apple Pudding

- 2 cups whole milk
- 1/2 cup granulated sugar

- 1/4 cup cornstarch
- 1/4 tsp salt
- 1 cup applesauce (unsweetened or lightly sweetened)
- 1/2 tsp vanilla extract
- 1/2 tsp ground cinnamon

Instructions:

1. **Mix Dry Ingredients:** In a medium saucepan, whisk together sugar, cornstarch, salt, and cinnamon.
2. **Combine Liquids:** Gradually whisk in milk until smooth.
3. **Cook Pudding:** Cook over medium heat, whisking constantly until the mixture thickens and starts to bubble (about 5-7 minutes).
4. **Add Applesauce and Vanilla:** Remove from heat and stir in applesauce and vanilla extract.
5. **Chill:** Pour into serving dishes and refrigerate for at least 2 hours before serving.

Cheesecake Pudding

- 2 cups whole milk
- 1/2 cup granulated sugar

- 1/4 cup cornstarch
- 1/4 tsp salt
- 1/2 cup cream cheese, softened
- 1/2 tsp vanilla extract
- 1/2 tsp lemon juice

Instructions:

1. **Mix Dry Ingredients:** In a medium saucepan, whisk together sugar, cornstarch, and salt.
2. **Combine Liquids:** Gradually whisk in milk until smooth.
3. **Cook Pudding:** Cook over medium heat, whisking constantly until the mixture thickens and starts to bubble (about 5-7 minutes).
4. **Add Cream Cheese, Vanilla, and Lemon Juice:** Remove from heat and stir in softened cream cheese, vanilla extract, and lemon juice until smooth.
5. **Chill:** Pour into serving dishes and refrigerate for at least 2 hours before serving.

Chocolate Mint Pudding

- 2 cups whole milk
- 1/2 cup granulated sugar
- 1/4 cup unsweetened cocoa powder

- 1/4 cup cornstarch
- 1/4 tsp salt
- 1/2 tsp mint extract
- 1/2 cup chocolate chips (optional)

Instructions:

1. **Mix Dry Ingredients:** In a medium saucepan, whisk together sugar, cocoa powder, cornstarch, and salt.
2. **Combine Liquids:** Gradually whisk in milk until smooth.
3. **Cook Pudding:** Cook over medium heat, whisking constantly until the mixture thickens and starts to bubble (about 5-7 minutes).
4. **Add Mint Extract and Chocolate:** Remove from heat and stir in mint extract and chocolate chips if using until melted and smooth.
5. **Chill:** Pour into serving dishes and refrigerate for at least 2 hours before serving.

Carrot Pudding

- 2 cups whole milk
- 1/2 cup granulated sugar
- 1/4 cup cornstarch

- 1/4 tsp salt
- 1 cup carrot puree (steamed and blended carrots)
- 1/2 tsp vanilla extract
- 1/2 tsp ground cinnamon

Instructions:

1. **Mix Dry Ingredients:** In a medium saucepan, whisk together sugar, cornstarch, salt, and cinnamon.
2. **Combine Liquids:** Gradually whisk in milk until smooth.
3. **Cook Pudding:** Cook over medium heat, whisking constantly until the mixture thickens and starts to bubble (about 5-7 minutes).
4. **Add Carrot Puree and Vanilla:** Remove from heat and stir in carrot puree and vanilla extract.
5. **Chill:** Pour into serving dishes and refrigerate for at least 2 hours before serving.

Fig Pudding

- 2 cups whole milk
- 1/2 cup granulated sugar
- 1/4 cup cornstarch

- 1/4 tsp salt
- 1 cup fig puree (made from cooked and blended figs)
- 1/2 tsp vanilla extract

Instructions:

1. **Mix Dry Ingredients:** In a medium saucepan, whisk together sugar, cornstarch, and salt.
2. **Combine Liquids:** Gradually whisk in milk until smooth.
3. **Cook Pudding:** Cook over medium heat, whisking constantly until the mixture thickens and starts to bubble (about 5-7 minutes).
4. **Add Fig Puree and Vanilla:** Remove from heat and stir in fig puree and vanilla extract.
5. **Chill:** Pour into serving dishes and refrigerate for at least 2 hours before serving.

Cherry Pudding

- 2 cups whole milk
- 1/2 cup granulated sugar
- 1/4 cup cornstarch
- 1/4 tsp salt

- 1 cup cherry puree (made from fresh or frozen cherries)
- 1/2 tsp vanilla extract

Instructions:

1. **Mix Dry Ingredients:** In a medium saucepan, whisk together sugar, cornstarch, and salt.
2. **Combine Liquids:** Gradually whisk in milk until smooth.
3. **Cook Pudding:** Cook over medium heat, whisking constantly until the mixture thickens and starts to bubble (about 5-7 minutes).
4. **Add Cherry Puree and Vanilla:** Remove from heat and stir in cherry puree and vanilla extract.
5. **Chill:** Pour into serving dishes and refrigerate for at least 2 hours before serving.

Date Pudding

- 2 cups whole milk
- 1/2 cup granulated sugar
- 1/4 cup cornstarch
- 1/4 tsp salt

- 1 cup date puree (made from soaked and blended dates)
- 1/2 tsp vanilla extract

Instructions:

1. **Mix Dry Ingredients:** In a medium saucepan, whisk together sugar, cornstarch, and salt.
2. **Combine Liquids:** Gradually whisk in milk until smooth.
3. **Cook Pudding:** Cook over medium heat, whisking constantly until the mixture thickens and starts to bubble (about 5-7 minutes).
4. **Add Date Puree and Vanilla:** Remove from heat and stir in date puree and vanilla extract.
5. **Chill:** Pour into serving dishes and refrigerate for at least 2 hours before serving.

Nutella Pudding

- 2 cups whole milk
- 1/2 cup Nutella
- 1/4 cup granulated sugar
- 1/4 cup cornstarch

- 1/4 tsp salt
- 1/2 tsp vanilla extract

Instructions:

1. **Mix Dry Ingredients:** In a medium saucepan, whisk together sugar, cornstarch, and salt.
2. **Combine Liquids:** Gradually whisk in milk until smooth.
3. **Cook Pudding:** Cook over medium heat, whisking constantly until the mixture thickens and starts to bubble (about 5-7 minutes).
4. **Add Nutella and Vanilla:** Remove from heat and stir in Nutella and vanilla extract until smooth.
5. **Chill:** Pour into serving dishes and refrigerate for at least 2 hours before serving.